REVELATION REVEALED

A GUIDE TO THE ENDTIMES AND THE APOCALYPSE

REV. DAVID D. COOK

Copyright © 2010 Rev. David D. Cook

All rights reserved. No part of this book may be used or reproduced by any means, graphic, electronic, or mechanical, including photocopying, recording, taping or by any information storage retrieval system without the written permission of the publisher except in the case of brief quotations embodied in critical articles and reviews.

Scripture taken from the King James Version of the Bible unless otherwise noted.

WestBow Press books may be ordered through booksellers or by contacting:

WestBow Press
A Division of Thomas Nelson
1663 Liberty Drive
Bloomington, IN 47403
www.westbowpress.com
1-(866) 928-1240

Because of the dynamic nature of the Internet, any Web addresses or links contained in this book may have changed since publication and may no longer be valid. The views expressed in this work are solely those of the author and do not necessarily reflect the views of the publisher, and the publisher hereby disclaims any responsibility for them.

ISBN: 978-1-4497-0457-5 (sc)
ISBN: 978-1-4497-0469-8 (e)

Library of Congress Control Number: 2010934081

Printed in the United States of America

WestBow Press rev. date: 9/13/2010

Contents

Introduction vii
Chapter 1 1
Chapter 2 7
Chapter 3 21
Finally 37
Appendix I 39
Appendix II 41
Appendix III 43
Appendix IV 45

Introduction

Revelation is a book both feared and revered by even the brightest and most educated Bible scholars. This study of the book of Revelation is written as a guide to the book as I understand it. You should come to your own conclusions in this study, and I expect that you will see things that I missed, and such should be the result of any study of Scripture. You should have a good working knowledge of the Scriptures before undertaking a study of Revelation, and I encourage any novice of the word to start their studies in the book of John. I would also recommend to you the reading of the entire Bible if you have not yet done this, as it is the least that any Christian should do considering the importance of this book to our faith. Many of the men who penned these books died as martyrs and outcasts, but you will only suffer a mild time inconvenience to accomplish what is the minimum for the study and discussion of any book.

You who are studying this book and have fit the minimum qualifications set forth will find that the view expressed is a little different than what you have probably been taught. I only ask that you give it an honest read. The desire of my heart is that you will come to your own conclusions, increase your faith in our Lord Jesus Christ, and draw closer to Him. If you are convinced to change your views based only on what I have said, you have missed the point. Trust God! Trust the Bible! Pray for His soon coming! These are all that I desire from you.

Chapter 1

Many have said that it is necessary to basically cut and paste Revelation into a proper order for it to make sense, but we do the Scripture an injustice when we make it fit our beliefs as opposed to simply changing our beliefs. The book is in logical order, and I believe that it is in chronological order, as it is expressed in Revelation 1:4. The real dispute occurs between three major Christian views of eschatology. These views vary from a strictly symbolic view, a historical view, and a futuristic view, and there are many who mix and match some of each of these, which probably will include most of us. Those who hold to a symbolic view generally teach that we cannot understand this book any other way, and those who teach it as historic generally agree that most of the events of Revelation are fulfilled prophecy to those who are currently alive. The futuristic view claims that most of the book is still unfulfilled prophecy. The big dividing line is the teaching of the "rapture of the church" and its time frame. I have dear friends who fall all over this spectrum of beliefs, and I believe them all to be genuine believers in Christ. I also can respect each one's view and have had some interesting and sometimes humorous discussions of this with them. You will probably find my views strange, as they do include aspects of each of these beliefs.

This book of the Bible is entitled "The Revelation of St. John the Divine" in most of the versions of the Bible I have seen. Chapter 1, however, starts with a different title, "The revelation of Jesus Christ, which God gave unto him …" which shows us not just that it was given to John by God but also that the revelation is of Jesus Christ. It is very important that we never lose sight of Jesus Christ in the study of this book or any book of the Bible. It is the doctrine of the Savior that separates the church from the cult. The titles given to Christ are also important. For example, being the Son of God as well as the Son of man is to be the set standard as well as the Savior of all who believe.

Verse 1 indicates that this prophecy is to be soon unfolding. In studying the prophecies in the rest of the Bible, we have seen that they are proven to be correct up to the current time. They all are fulfilled as they claim. Time is an earthly concept that was established in the creation, and we also know that time is relative from 2 Peter 3:8, where we are told that a thousand years is as a day with God. God is not encumbered with our estimation of time. The grand scheme of things is beyond us, before us, and after us and this earth. We are told that this prophecy must soon come to pass. In chapter 22, we are told by Christ that He will come quickly, and John agrees that he is ready for His return. He has not yet returned; therefore, we can assume that He is closer now than ever before. This is given as an encouragement to John and should be to us also.

In verse 2, we discover that John is to bear record of three things in this book. First, he establishes this as the word of God. Second, he gives us the testimony of Jesus Christ to give credence to this claim. Third, he gives his own eyewitness account of both of these. A careful study of the prophets, the life of Christ, and the character of John establishes the three-pointed plane upon which we can solidly build. Therefore, we are encouraged to build using three points for stability. We are then given a threefold blessing for reading, understanding, and keeping (holding to, performing) the things that are written therein. We are then reminded of His soon coming. It is a shame that so many neglect the reading of the Bible when such a blessing is given on this the final book of Scripture.

Pretribulationists make up most of the futuristic camp of eschatologists. Verse 4 carries the weightiest part of their stance.

This is their way of bringing logic to the timeline of this book. It is better for us to use verse 4 as a continuing theme and reference to Jesus Christ. The number seven begins its theme here as well. It is the number of churches and the number of spirits here. There are some who apply numerology to the Bible. For example, the number seven is to them the number of completeness, beginning with God's seven-day creation of the Earth and all that it is in it. While this may hold some truth, we should not base our doctrines on numerology. We should base it on "rightly dividing" the Scripture. Seven is commonly used to show completeness, but in the book of Revelation, it runs through the whole. This book is the representation of the last age of earth. It is the book of the end times. The word "spirit" is translated from the word that means breath or wind. It is the giver of life and the making of motion in those who allow this in their lives. God breathed life into man. Ephesians 4:14 tells us not to be moved by every wind of doctrine. In light of this, it behooves us to establish fact as opposed to being moved by what just sounds good. If we properly apply verse 4, we will find grace and peace in heeding the warnings that this book provides.

Jesus Christ is introduced in verse 5 with three defining characteristics. Once again, it is easy to take the numerology of three being a divine number. Remember, though, we are here to discover, not to apply "winds of doctrine," as we are told in Ephesians 4:14. This theme of three is found also throughout the Bible and especially in this book. We have already seen the three of "Him which is, and which was, and which is to come," and the three-pointed blessing for our study and application of this book. This theme is almost hidden in the background as we read while the sevens are in plain view. We find that Christ is three things as the faithful witness (Heb. 7:25), the first begotten of the dead (1 Cor. 15:20), and the prince of the kings of the earth (Rom. 14:11). These statements are used for our Heavenly Father in the previous verse. Christ is presently the witness (Heb. 7:25). He is the first and only begotten and like a prince is waiting for God to exalt Him to the undisputed position of authority above all. We all know that He has no beginning or ending. These "kings of the Earth" (Rev. 20:6) are to soon lose their positions. He loves us (present), He washed us (past), and He made us kings and priests (future Rev. 20:6).

Verse 9 introduces us to John. He here appeals to our brotherhood with him. John tells us that he was "in the Spirit on the Lord's Day," and we should understand that to us, every day should be the Lord's. John, while in the Spirit, hears a "great voice, as of a trumpet." A trumpet is used to sound battle instructions to the troops (1 Cor. 14:8) as well as to herald incoming royalty. Jesus then introduces Himself accordingly as "Alpha and Omega, the first and the last" (John 1). John is then told to write what he sees, which becomes very important later in the study. Jesus also tells him how this letter is to be addressed and sent.

In verses 12 through 18, we begin to see the permeation of the number seven and a detailed description of Jesus Christ. The symbolism of these verses can be lost in our feelings, and John is probably stricken by this sight, as we would be. We are in this study speaking the obvious and leaving the feelings to the reader. There are seven candlesticks burning in the presence of Christ. These are lamp stands. Olive oil was used with a wick to produce a burning light in this type of stand, and olive oil is nearly always symbolic of the Spirit of God. Lamps were used to illuminate the darkness and as a guiding point in the night. We then see a description of the speaker as given by John, who had personally known Jesus, as like unto the Son of man. The rest of the description is striking and symbolic to those who read it. There are as many opinions of the symbolism as there are students of Revelation. I think that this is the point of the description. We see Jesus as what He is in our mind and heart. Jesus is always found complete, the first and last, as well as the beginning and the end. We see that beside His appearance, He speaks with a voice that is like many waters sounding. There are many references to water in the Scriptures that make this trait significant: the Spirit moved on the face of the water at the creation, the water of the Red Sea parted, the water flowed from the rock, the water of the Jordan parted, the water covered the earth in the flood, the water that would have cooled the tongue of the rich man, the water that baptizes, and the water of life. Jesus holds in His hand seven stars. We are told in Genesis that stars mark time. We know by practice that they are used for navigation. Out of His mouth proceeds a sharp, two-edged sword, which we know from Hebrews 4:12–13 divides rightly all things and makes all things naked and open in His sight. His countenance was so bright that John fell at His feet as dead. This is not surprising, as John was but a man and Jesus divine.

After we are introduced to Jesus, we begin to see, hear, and understand. Jesus touches John with his right hand, which formerly held the stars. Paul wrote to Timothy of the gift that was imparted by the laying on of his hands. We should expect infinitely more from Christ as His hand that holds the messages is laid upon the messenger (vs. 20). John is instructed not to fear, which can come only from the redemption of Jesus Christ. He is told again that He is the "first and last." An interesting subject and verb combination of "I AM" is found here. This contains a thought of self-existence. He exists beyond and apart from the universe. Where I can say, "I am a preacher," it is dependent upon my preaching. "I am human" is dependent upon having human parents. To be "first and last" in a cosmic sense is to be "before and after" all that exists. He is self-defined, which is something that we can never be as created beings. A study of the life of Moses will bear this out in the first as this does in the last. He is ever-present, not just eternal. This is continued in verse 18. He is presently alive forever. Even in physical death, He is alive. He presently holds the keys of death and hell forever.

In verse 19, John is again instructed to write the things that he has seen, the things that are now and the things that shall be here after. Another triplet is given for the things John should write, and it matches the core triplet of Christ, which as we remember Christ says that He is that "which is, and which was, and which is to come." We will see the triplet apply in the letters to the churches. This past to present shift can indicate to us the nature of Christ. The sin of my past is presently before Him unless it is covered by Christ's blood, which is eternal. We were saved, are saved, and yet are to be saved.

Chapter 2

Chapter 2 of the book of Revelation also marks the second division of our study. The instructions given to John in the previous chapter are important to the proper reading and understanding of these seven churches. The direction given to John is to write past, present, and future. Each church should be read with each inflection. There are three messages in each church, tying each of the three major schools of thought together. We must read these letters as separate epistles to each of these seven churches. This would be a past view to those of us who are now living as well as to John once they have left his hands. We also must read them as inspired Scripture. This makes them presently demanding upon us to keep and perform their lessons. They are also to have a future view in them. There have been several schools of thought with this in mind that have termed these as church ages. I agree that this is a valid thought. It is, however, in applying all three views that we fulfill the responsibility as a reader and student of this book. This type of study causes a completion that is inferred in chapter 1 verses 5–7, 8, 12, 16, and 19–20. These verses are immersed in the concepts of seven and three (past, present, and future). We should not, as I have said before, start blindly throwing numerological values on everything, but we should use their thematic virtue as a glue to bind us together upon the more important principles of being Christians. The views of the timing of or the existing of rapture for the church are not nearly as important as the simpler fact that God is the judge and before Him we all must go. This is true regardless of when and how we get there. We may all have a personal rapture called death.

The word angel is simply the messenger to each respective church. This was either an elder or bishop in the local congregation much the same as pastors, preachers, bishops, or whomever your particular group uses to instruct your local body of believers. Some have asserted that these were literal, heaven-sent angels that were at each church, but the instructions given to Timothy as to the structure and qualifications of the leadership of the church at Ephesus do not bear this out as plausible. As much as possible, we need to let the Holy Spirit direct us in our reading of this book. We do not need to use my views as inspired writing. When you took it upon yourself to study this book, you became your own angel because you are the one reading, just as those leaders did for their many times unlearned congregations who did not own a New Testament, as it did not yet exist. I am certain that all seven churches received a physical letter from John. I am certain also that the Spirit intends for us to apply the messages of these churches to ourselves. The prophetic, however, is to be seen through the aid of the sevenfold Spirit of God to whom we were introduced in 1:4. It is not a multitude of gods but rather a logical progression that is found between these churches' problems and their relationship one to another.

Beginning in the church at Ephesus, let us keep ourselves centered in the reality of each church's first-century epistle (our past) and our church's epistle of inspired Scripture (our present). After this, we will approach the prophetic as best as we can. Ephesus has Christ introduced to them from the description in chapter 1. Any epistle should by its nature have an introduction, and Christ is dictating while John is writing. We can assume that the Ephesian church was familiar with the Savior. This is a credit to Timothy and the church for having heeded the Pauline epistle written to them about thirty years previous. They tried the false teachers that were plaguing them and continued in their works, labor, and patience. The first love of the church is somehow forgotten, however. This is a negative mark for them (verse 5). In verse six, we find a positive to them in that they hate the deeds of the Nicolaitans. This word literally means followers of Nicholas, but it is inferred in the name a meaning of a heretical teaching of subduing the laity (people of the church not in leadership). This heresy is still found where the laity does not personally take responsibility to search out the Scriptures for the purpose of self-betterment but also to assure that heresy is not taught in their church by one claiming to be the oracle of God. This heresy is always for the purpose of imposing power over the church for the leader's benefit. Ephesians 1 shows us that the church's first love is Christ. All these glorious attributes of Christ described in Revelations 2:1 are a reminder to the Ephesians of their first love, much like describing the object of your first love to you years after you last beheld his or her beauty.

The present church, our church, has the same sort of issues as Ephesus. As God is unchanging, we should handle these problems in the way prescribed at Ephesus. We find the solution to this found in the book of the Ephesians, 1 and 2 Timothy, and here in the book of Revelation. If we would start performing as these texts explain to us that we should, our churches would break out into a true revival. We have prayed for this revival for years, but we have not been faithful to the word. Counterfeit revivals spring up from heretical teaching and make it impossible for true revival to be experienced on the large scale. It is not God's fault but our own. "He that hath an ear let him hear what the Spirit saith to the churches," is told to the reader or hearer of this letter, not just Ephesus. The blessing is to him who "overcometh," which is the "keeping" of chapter 1. The overcomer is seen eating of the tree of life in the midst of the paradise of God. Sadly, we see a demise of the light at Ephesus. There are still churches in the area around Ephesus. Christianity survives, but what would it have been if they had overcome? The Ephesian church age has passed, and we will look at that closer as we progress through the letters.

Smyrna also receives an introduction of Christ. Once again, it would have been obvious to one who truly knew the character of the Lord. Our hope as Christians rests hard upon the fact of Christ's deity, and we find alluded to in that He is the "first and last." Our hope also rests upon the perfect sacrifice that He made and is proven by His first fruit resurrection, which is covered in His statement "was dead, and is alive." This to me is like a cool drink of water to one walking in the desert. We see that there are works at Smyrna, but it also has tribulation and poverty. This is a change from what was found in Ephesus. Smyrna's works are not coupled with labor and patience. This pain is to continue unto death, but ultimately the faithful will receive a crown of life. There is no mention of correction to this problem, but there is encouragement given that it will not follow past the grave.

We are beginning to see tribulation to the believer here in the United States but not anything like what Smyrna was experiencing. We now must remember who and what Jesus is to us if we are to remain strong through the hard times that may lie before us. Things can change quickly, but God never changes. The concept of church ages is that Ephesus was representative of the earliest form of the church, and Smyrna is representative of the church during the great persecutions. This progression of thought is natural in the light of the geographic, political, and judicial nearness of the seven churches one to another. The climate contained in these three bonds is extremely different from Ephesus to Smyrna. This makes us ask how this could be. We'll continue this after Pergamus.

A most disturbing introduction of the Lord is given to the church at Pergamus. We know from other studies of the New Testament that the sharp, two-edged sword is the word of God, and we find that it is in the mouth of the Lord in chapter 1. We must understand as Christians that the things that proceed from the mouth of God are always powerful. We should not take the word of God lightly, ever, not just when it is manifested to us as a sword! The use of the sword is interesting due to its use as a representative of justice as well as its use as an offensive weapon. It was the spoken word of God that formed this universe and all that in it is. It should never be neglected. Works are here mentioned again. This church has an established dwelling place, and within it Satan has his own seat. On a very simplistic level, many churches have people who are more interested in if someone is going to take their seat from them than they are about the day's worship and message. Many have those who are more concerned about their position in the church than the purpose of the position. Many denominations recognize the authority of a man as the oracle or the mouthpiece of God. These people often have positions that are referred to as a seat, chair, or sitting person. Sometimes they sit in a chair within the walls of an edifice and call that physical seat a cathedra. Using these titles for these people and their parking place does not necessarily make one Satan, but we can see how Satan's place in the church can be easily called his seat. It is scary to think that Satan can be this deceiving, or that he should be so comfortable in our churches that he would be willing to sit down and take a rest. Pergamus had a faithful servant slain at Satan's bidding within the church. How many were slain at the instruction of the Pope in the inquests? Many of them were killed for believing that salvation came by grace, through faith, and not at the hands or blessing of man. A faithful martyr is the only positive light shown in this church. How sad!

This church did have plenty negatives that were to be mentioned. The doctrine of Balaam is bringing much worldliness into the church. The doctrine of the Nicolaitans is present here in Pergamus. This church is told to repent before the foundation of the church becomes a judge against her. How sad that Christ, who died for this church, now has to stand against it. The church had become a monster. Even sadder is that those who shall receive the promise are instructed that they are to come out from within this body. Manna is offered to nourish those who will leave, and a new name will be given in purity and secret to those who would depart the Pergamus church. We should accept the promise of hope for those who will stand against evil, even in the church.

The church age line now becomes more complicated. We now have two churches in the earth, one that is made up of those continuing to be deceived by the devil and one composed of those who came out and started over. The beginning of some who are Nicolaitane to a full doctrine of Nicolaitanism is apparent. The one church's government is wholly established in this doctrine, and the other is embarking on a perilous individual journey that is protected by God but must be done mostly in secret due to the great risk of offending the leader of the "organization" that we call the Pergamus church age and having to suffer martyrdom, as did Antipas, not at the hands of the Romans but the church's. This age is until the beginning of Protestantism.

Verse 18 brings us Thyatira. This church no longer recognizes Christ. They are bluntly told that it is Christ who speaks to them. The fire of His eyes brings us to remembrance of the method by which all of our works would be tried. His feet being of fine brass indicate the purity found in Christ's trial by fire. Works, as always, are mentioned. The church seems to always be busy with something but seldom with what is right. There is no way that any Christian, whether by name or in truth, can have zero works. We all are doing works whether right or wrong, but we are nonetheless doing works. Not even our idle thoughts and deeds are missed by the all-seeing, all-knowing, and all-present God we serve. The Thyatira works list begins well. Charity, service, faith, patience, and work (labor) start us out. This all sounds good and wholesome. Work is mentioned twice (more at the latter than at the first). We should, however, not forget that we are saved by grace through faith, not of works, lest any man should boast. This should sound familiar to the Bible student. Despite what seemed to be a super-positive start, verse 20 starts with the word "notwithstanding" (contrariwise). Good works, deeds, religion, and endurance can never outweigh sin. Sin has to be confessed, not covered (1 John 1:9–10). Once inside Thyatira, we find that which was a teaching in verse 14 has become a practice in 20. This again shows a logical progression that even if not establishing this church-age belief that we are discussing, does tell us that we must be careful as to what teaching we allow in our churches. Verse 21 shows us the forgiving nature of Jesus, but 22 reveals the result of refusal, even to tribulation.

Starting now in verse 24, a remnant of believers is found. They have nothing to do with the depth of Satan. What had previously been the seat of Satan has grown deep. It has rooted itself into the very core of the church like a cancer. This remnant is instructed to hold fast and they will receive power. In verses 27–28, this promise takes form. We must understand that Jezebel was a feared manipulator of much wickedness. She stood against and murdered the prophets of the Most High, who were the only ones standing for truth. There is one major group that reveres the presence and instruction of a female entity. This was framed during a most powerful time in church history. Power is a reward only to those who have no power in their current situation. This remnant is formed of those who once had the kiss of Jezebel's approval but now stand against the direction of that organization by protesting the rule of Satan within its structure. This doesn't mean that there is no salvation even near the depth of Satan, but this does mean that the blessings of God have departed and are found with those who are willing to stand apart from this travesty of church and suffer accordingly if necessary to please God.

The beginning of chapter 3 brings with it a divergence of paths for some of our differing systems of eschatological view. I have friends, brothers in the Lord, who differ with me on my views up to this point. I have some who have continued with me until now but will soon depart. I also have some who believe here as I do. This is to be expected amongst those who do study for themselves the prophecies of the Bible. It is beyond rare that two individuals even from within the same frame of belief will agree on everything within it. Most who completely agree with others did not study the Scriptures but rather the teachings of the person they are agreeing with. I respectfully disagree with teachers, writers, and Christian celebrities who have more education, credentials, and backing than I have, as well as some who are just as common as me. This separation occurs at the church age level at this point. I still maintain that the epistle nature of this part of Revelations is of the utmost importance to us as Christians. We should not disagree on that point. We all need to examine ourselves and our churches to make sure that we are not yielding to the influences of Satan upon us. Eschatologically, we need to respect the differences and focus on the commission of Christ. The ultimate end to all eschatology should be that Christ is soon returning, regardless of what our personal calendars may contain, and upon this return judgment will begin whether before

Christ or the White Throne. We need to be faithful to the end, whenever that may be.

Sardis seems to be a church system with little or no hope. There is found no real redeeming quality for this church. It is of great interest that the introduction of Christ has Him holding the message (spirits) and the messengers (stars). As with all these epistles, the introduction says much about the health of the church to which it is addressed. The control of the message and messenger should never leave the hands of Christ. Sardis is simply told that their works were resulting in a living and yet dead situation. In the book of 2 Timothy 3:5, we find that in the last days there will be messengers who will have a form of godliness but deny its power. We were instructed in that book to turn away from such. Living and yet being dead indicates formal religion without personal salvation. At all costs, we need to avoid this in our churches if we are to please God. In verse 3, Sardis is told that if they will not change, the hour will come upon them while they are unaware. In verse 4, it is worse when we find that only a few of its members find a personal relationship with Christ. Salvation has never come with formal church membership and never will. The thought that the coming of Christ will take this church unaware signifies that we have reached the final three church ages. If we were to go back to Genesis and use a calculator for the ages of deaths of the antediluvian fathers, we would find that Methuselah died the year of the flood, as well as all those after him, except, of course, Noah and his descendents. The same holds true for these last three churches. Sardis is an extension from Thyatira. Philadelphia extends from the remnant and represents true Christianity, not cold, dead religion. Laodicea will be an extension of Sardis, the unrepentant.

Philadelphia literally means brotherly love. This church is to me the most positive of the seven. The introduction of our savior is of the attributes of His nature and authority. He is holy, and we know Him as such due to the proof of His resurrection. He is true due to His holiness bearing out His word and law. He holds the key of David, the beloved. "This is my beloved Son in whom I am well pleased." This key is important and will be a continuing theme.

This key makes it possible for Him to open and close in a humanly impossible way. Beyond this lovely introduction is the message to this church. He mentions their works as usual. Nothing more is mentioned about them, and the focus then returns to Christ. The church is instructed on the status of a door. Christ alone controls this status and has opened it. We must continue on until we cross that threshold. The works then are revisited as the reason for the door having been opened for this church. Strength here denotes the miraculous strength that comes only through Christ. His word is kept, and His name not denied.

Now we can step a little further into the three different prophetic views. At the time of this letter, we can assume that the church at Philadelphia is about the Lord's work. If we make an application of this letter to our present church, we can see that in working for Christ, we will have those miracles that expedite His work. If we fulfill the word in light of the introduction of Christ as holy and true, we must confess Him alone as Savior, Lord, brother, intercessor, way, truth, and life. He alone is worthy for glory. His crown is not shared by His mother, apostles, angels, priests, laws, rituals, or anyone else. This is an opposite teaching from the Nicolaitanes and other entities of the previous churches. This true placing of Christ should be at the forefront of true Christianity.

We find some negatives in verse 9, but they apply to some in the church and not the church as a whole. There are some who say that they are Jews and are not. The word Jews here is not synonymous with Israelite but means "to be of Judah." Judah as a name is "celebrated." We need to remember that the names of Bible times had common meaning. Judah was person, place, and a concept. They were those who claimed to be Jews inside of the church and were not were heaped into an assembly (synagogue) of Satan. There is apparently a struggle going on between these factions. Jesus will set it right at His coming. Due to the positive of verse 8, a promise as opposed to a judgment is given to this church at verse 10. This "word" is an enormous base of definition that leads us to an understanding that Christ's "word of His patience" is the drive of our work. His patience is a "cheerful endurance." We may here simplify this with the example of the mind-set of a child waiting on Christmas morning. Christ left us with a command to seek the lost. He longs to return but patiently waits on the command of the Father. We long for His return, and to demonstrate this, we should be busy accomplishing the things He asks us to do, which is the seeking of the lost. This work comes from a personal relationship and personal knowledge of Jesus Christ and not just the assembly of celebration, which is ritualistic and leads the lost not to Christ but to a "salvation" of association and performance. This all applies to both the church at Philadelphia and to our present church

It has proved impossible for me to find a way to link this epistle's promise of the hour of temptation for the whole world and to a church that physically was written to in the first century other than through the concept of the church age. This statement of promise in verse 10 is a major foundation for the pretribulational and midtribulational rapture teachings. In this study, we sought to establish that Philadelphia was formed of those who came out from among the church at Thyatira and its false teaching. It is this fork in the road that brings us to the diversity of teaching that is seen in the church today. We should all have garnered an understanding that we should establish the right doctrines and avoid the evils of these epistles. Christ is for all who will believe, but each individual is responsible to believe on Him alone. For instance, if your church is teaching worldliness, subjection of the laity, multiple ways of salvation, works as a way of salvation, sexual immorality, or that Christ has already returned, you have the duty to correct this, even if this means that you leave that church and find one that is not heretical. Those who can sit idly by while these things are falsely taught or those who cheerfully conform to these false teachings constitute the age of Sardis, and those who hold to Christ alone are Philadelphia.

Looking again at the promise of verse 10, we see the hope contained in some of the theories. These individuals who make up the church at Philadelphia are raptured, covered, and shielded in place, or die all previous to the wrath of God being poured out on the whole earth in what is generally called the "Great Tribulation."

I will not go into great detail and depth with the Old Testament prophecies of Daniel and Ezekiel, as they are both prophetic to the Israelites and largely finished in those prophecies. We as the church are to be considered among the Gentile or Greek world as well as being Christians. It never does one any good to place oneself into the wrong set of prophecy. I will use mostly if not entirely New Testament sources to help us to understand that there is a difference between these two lines of prophecy. I know that some who are reading this are thinking back to studies in your past where you were taught the prophecies of Daniel with the book of Revelation. That is all right if done properly. If I were to say to my son that he will be getting a vehicle from me in the future, that does not mean that you would necessarily get one also. All the Bible's prophecies, when properly researched, do provide support to each other, but most of the prophecies of Daniel were filled in Antiochus Epiphanies and do not need then to be filled again. There is a shadowing or mirroring of these events in the book of Revelation, but they are in application to the entire world. I still respect those who have diligently studied in that way. Many of them would do me shame in their knowledge of those books, and they may be right. I disagree with their conclusion, and I love them just the same. We should all agree on the primary need to be good stewards of the time that we have regardless of how it shall end. It was being a good steward that will make and has made Philadelphia great.

    Verse 11 reiterates the never-changing fact that Christ is soon to come. In 1 Corinthians 15:52, it states that it shall be "in the twinkling of an eye." This denotes not just when but how He comes. At a speed of sixty miles per hour, a checkpoint that is one mile away is also just one minute away. If a man is standing at that checkpoint awaiting our passing but is occupied with other things so that he is not looking down the road in the direction that we shall come and is listening to an engrossing conversation and not listening for the sound of the road, the passing of the car will take him so unaware that the car will be by him before he can distinguish the face of the driver. Christ's coming shall be the same. As we are told in 2 Timothy 4:8 that we should love His appearing. This occupies our mind with the driver and directs our eyes toward Him. We must hold fast in the light of His soon coming. We should love and not smite His servants. The overcoming principle in verse 12 consists of beautiful promises. We will see the promises in detail later. The overcomer from the church at Philadelphia finds his reward in the things of the very end, the final things. This fact is curiously used by some of all the views of eschatology as a profound proof of their stance. I will just thank God for the reward. I really don't deserve one.

Finally, in this list of seven churches comes Laodicea. This church is viewed differently from one belief system to another and often even between individuals within a group. In this study we will continue to focus on Christ and church. Christ is introduced to this church as a stranger would be introduced. The attributes used in chapter 1 are not used here. No physical description is mentioned. He is introduced in an abrupt fashion. This is how He will be returning, also. The beginning of this epistle is similar to an ending, as "amen" is not usually a greeting. Amen, so be it, is now the name used for Christ. This is used by some who take the premillenial stance to establish the time of the rapture. Any way you choose to look at this, regardless of eschatological view, take notice of the profound lack of any positive thing said of this church. A child who has pushed an authority figure to the edge may hear something like, "All right! Enough! So be it! That is it!" Jesus is also introduced as faithful and true as a witness, and the beginning of the creation of God. He is not a newcomer, but rather, He predates all of this that we know as creation.

Laodicea as a church hears the same as the rest of the churches, that Christ knows their works. Once again, this can be either good or bad. Christ knows ours as well. Nothing is hidden from the eyes of Christ. Laodicea is neither hot nor cold. Christ would rather it be one or the other. I have heard several people comment on this and am inclined to believe that it has to do with a mixing of thought and deed in an unholy way much like mixing hot and cold water. Hot water cleanses and cold water refreshes, but the mixture of the two does neither, and in fact creates an environment that breeds disease.

This is disgusting and stomach turning. If my actions and words have the wrong motivation mixed with them, it works the same. He who "loveth and telleth a lie" is disgusting in a spiritual way to the point of exclusion (Rev. 22:15). For a person to perform hyper religious ritual to show *his or her* godliness and live worldly to satisfy *his or her* lust is a disgusting mix that breeds spiritual disease. In verse 17, we see that Laodicea is wealthy. They were even able to forgo political financial help after a devastating earthquake destroyed the city. The mind-set of their self-sufficiency overflowed into the church. They could not or would not see that their prosperity and all that it makes available does not constitute righteousness before God. Christ tells them that in His eyes that they were anything but prosperous. They were then dirty but thought themselves clean, cold but thought themselves to be hot, and blind but thought they could see. Jesus counsels them to buy of Him gold tried in the fire that they might be truly rich. We know that this is impossible. You cannot buy anything from Christ because it is free to the asking. Our riches then are not able to establish spirituality. This church did not know Christ. They were relying on self. The white raiment is an emblem of purity, and the eye salve is a play against the livelihood of the Laodicean community. Jesus is making it clear that the going through with the motions is not a substitute for relationship with Him but rather being lukewarm. In verse 19, we see that those who are loved of Christ are rebuked and chastened. In verses 20–22, we understand that the admonition given herein is to the individual, not the collective.

Most of the people who are of church age thinking believe that each church is a separate period in time. Most think that they belong to one the two final churches. We have begun to explore the possibility that church age thinking could also lead us to the conclusion that just before Christ's return there will be three churches represented. None of the previous ages went out with an announcement to the world that they were changing ages. It happens gradually with overlapping time. In the end, however, there are three. Sardis and Philadelphia are waning. Laodicea with her prosperity doctrines easily looks like our word of faith and financial seed movements of the day with their fixation on physical health and financial wealth. Philadelphia exists today as the true church of the individually redeemed and concerned of their good works and brotherly love. Sardis exists at this time as the ritualistic church. However, after the time of the rapture, Laodicea will be the only church left. It will absorb Sardis in the absence of Philadelphia as the evils of the previous church always morph into the next generation of church. This is not elitist, as there will be the individuals who have received Christ from both Sardis and Laodicea who will be raptured, and Philadelphia exists only of the saved. Your local congregation does not make up Philadelphia. You do! A person can attend the wrong congregation but have personal relationship with Christ. This finishes the view of the church, but the prophecy is to also the heavens and the earth.

Chapter 3

Revelation 4:1 is the classic foothold for the premillenial teacher to place the weight of a pretribulational stance. This has been popularized by several teachers over the last several years. It sounds good to any of us that we are out of here before anything bad really gets started. Most of this teaching bases itself on the quality of Christian life in the United States. Many scholars say that John is the representative of the church and that where he is we as the church must be. This cannot be backed in the book of Revelation as fact, and I intend to show that it is not case.

Some claim that the voice sounding like a trumpet is the trumpet call of the rapture of the saints, but there are many sounding voices and trumpets. Many place a great deal of emphasis on the word "hereafter" as an indicator of the rapture being past, but this, though intriguing, is really too heavy for this one word to support. I hope that I am totally wrong about the following view for my comfort and wellbeing as well as the church's ease of mind. I just don't think that I am. I would love to be going through a trouble-free, sunshiny day and just pop out of here and into heaven to be with Christ. That would be a glorious end to my time here on this earth as we now know it. The amillenialist believes it just means a continuation of later time. I am premillenial, but I do not believe for a moment that this is the rapture of the church. This voice, whether trumpeting or not, does not call the church up but rather the viewpoint of the prophet. It is not important where John is to the relationship of the location of the church.

As we have progressed through this, I have said and will continue to repeat that I think we all have a touch of correctness to our beliefs, but sensationalism and cold stonewalling does not help the plight of the church. "Hereafter" carries a view of where as well as when. The voice was from heaven; therefore, it stands to reason that the "here" part to us is really "there." The "after" part is related to the completion of this prophecy. Things occur not just on the earth but as we have seen previously in the worshipping of the beasts and elders, in heaven, also. While these churches are dealing with their personal problems, and while the church ages roll on by, heaven is alive with things to do because promises have been made. The viewpoint has changed from earth current to heaven current.

We need to stress and repeat here that the prophetic key should be in past, present, and future. Chapter 4 is loaded with this concept. Heaven changes little even during this book of prophecy. The twenty-four elders are always in some form of worship, the throne of God is always there, the sea of glass is always tranquil, and the four beasts don't leave. This cannot be said of the earth, however. Much debate occurs between most teachers of eschatology about the four beasts, the twenty-four elders, and God's throne. This is usually over who is in heaven at this time and who is not, which is to place a timeframe for the rapture or judgments of God. This to me is weak for timing, but tremendously important to the understanding of the nature of God. His heaven and kingdom operate outside of and regardless to our petty and insignificant thoughts and ideas. At the beginning of the earth this was the nature of heaven, timeless and peaceful. When this world ends, this nature remains, as God is unchanging. The wording of worship differs from place to place but is constant. The throne of God is unchanged, but the spatial relationship of man to it changes. The beasts, regardless of who or what they are, say, "Holy, holy, holy, Lord God Almighty, which was, which is, and is to come." This places heavenly worship into the very key of prophecy (past, present, and future). This is tremendous in understanding God. We see that when the beasts are silent that the twenty-four elders reply, "Thou art worthy, O Lord, to receive glory, and honor, and power: for thou hast created all things, and for thy pleasure they are and were created." The threefold is everywhere in these quotes.

The beginning of chapter 5 brings us to the widely known seven-sealed scroll. This scroll and the beliefs that surround it go outside of Christianity itself. The secular market for entertainment, the occultists, and even the plain superstitious love to talk about what it is. In our Christian circles of belief it varies just as much as in the world. I also find it interesting that any Christian can argue against the trinity in light of three clear passages of Scripture of which this is one. God, the Father, is sitting upon His throne holding this scroll in His right hand. In verse 7, He hands it to Christ, His son. In verse 6, the Spirit is referenced as "in the world." This is a beautiful representation of the Holy Trinity. Their relationship is perfectly unified though exclusive one from another. If you gather nothing in addition to the doctrine of the trinity, you will receive the promised blessing from chapter 1. This is a scroll that needs to be opened. It will require the hands of one who has been proven worthy, and despite what Hollywood thinks is entertaining, no one but Christ can open it. It is sealed on the back seven times. This makes the scroll impossible to open until all seven seals are opened. It is not as I have heard it so many times that one seal opens and a little rolling and reading is done. They are all exterior and thus must bind one large and important work. Christ's worthiness alone leads us to the fact that it predates mankind itself because the Lamb is slain from the foundations of the earth. Whether or not this scroll is a physical or symbolic thing is another argument that we can put to rest. It does not matter. Christ is worthy alone! Due to this worthiness, the very ones who were worshipping God are now praising Christ, and God is not jealous of this. This proves the deity of Christ (another blessing for studying).

The relationship of heaven to earth is brought to light in chapter 6. We are a conceited bunch that honestly believes that we can dictate morality, and that we are safe because of military might, and that money is wealth. The events surrounding this seven-sealed scroll will cause an adjustment in this way of thinking for those who will receive it. We must not, however, attribute the wrath of God to the seals of the scroll. That will come a little later. We do find that these seven seals show a logical order in their events. There are once again many opinions of these events, but we still endeavor to keep ourselves rooted in the key as we study. Christ is opening the seals individually and closing none. All the earth is affected by this progression. I hope that none have been so lulled to sleep by the easy out promised to them at the teaching of an earlier rapture. Times will be hard as they have been before. The church is already tortured in this world. We have it easy in the United States. Jesus Christ taught us that the world should hate us as it hated Him. If we are looking for the rapture, we are looking for a thief in the night (quiet, quick, and unannounced).

There is much anticipation of the opening of this scroll. Once the first seal opens, it is heralded by a thunderous voice that directs John to come and see, which means to beware. This is a rather bold beginning for the ending. The first beast is a reference to the beast in chapter 4 that was like a lion, the king of the beasts. He directs John to beware in coming and seeing. Why would one in the protection of the height of heaven need to beware of what is on the earth? This should cause one to think about the actual position of the church at this time. You have to beware (a warning) of things that can affect you. When this seal opens, a person riding a white horse appears. This horse represents the speed at which he may move, the color represents his perceived righteousness, and his bow indicates his ability to fight at a distance, thus maintaining his personal protection. He wears a crown, thus indicating that he is a political or civil leader of man. His work is in constant and mobile warfare. This we have seen at many times in the history of the world, but as technology of war has improved, it is more common now and will become even more common. Notice the use of the prophetic key. It fits the lock and will fit better as we progress.

The second seal has no bold exclamation in its opening. It is a logical progression from the first seal. The horse is red, which for the sake of sensationalism, is flame in color. Interestingly, he has the power to bring terror upon the earth. He has no crown to show him forth as a civil leader but still possesses influence enough to cause men to kill each other. This is coupled with the lack of the impersonal bow that strikes from a safe location and the addition of the sword, which is by nature personal in its use. The wielder of a sword is at the front of the battle and most times suffers or dies as a result. The beast in the second seal is like a calf, which is to the Middle Eastern cultures a sacrifice of some form of appeasement to some god.

The third seal is opened also with the same warning as the first two. A black horse carries this event, and black nearly always represents evil and calamity. He carries an even deadlier weapon than the first two. He carries balances. These are used in trade, commerce, and economics. He brings famine to the world due to financial recession or depression. A day's labor will buy only one day's ration of grain for one person. Prices are determined by man as well as interest rates and availability of work. How then shall the young, sick, old, and unskilled survive? Debt ensues from these situations and is not uncommon among those who have exhausted their resources in fighting constant war and terrorism. There is also a famine of the oil and wine. These products are produced by the labor of man upon a raw substance and are used for food, fuel, and medicine. This is truly a great worldwide famine that will touch all the common man.

The fourth beast (eagle) heralds in seal number four. The eagle is mentioned in Matthew 24 as gathering to the carcass. We are once again warned as to the coming rider who is upon a pale horse. Pale is the color of sickness and death. We are told that this rider is called Death and Hell. He is not referred to as a man but as a being. He is a thing that just is. One fourth of the population of the earth dies from the sword, hunger, dying, and the beasts of the earth. Simply, these people die as a result of the three riders and the progression of their work on earth as well as the unbalance in nature that ensues when man encroaches upon nature and destroys the natural balance. This can be seen throughout the history of the world, but each growing event makes it more global. For instance, this can be as simple as President George Bush beginning what could be seen as a righteous war to free the Kuwaitis from the aggression of Iraq's leadership. This results in a later response as a suicidal terrorist attack on the United States in the name of a holy war so called by their religious leaders. This causes the new civil leader of the United States, President George W. Bush, to expand this war against terror, which includes more nations. The two spirits of civil and religious warfare continue to fight while the entire world falls into unrest and terror. The result is a naturally unhealthy environment for sustained individual financial growth and leads to a worldwide recession. Recession brings with it less available resources and less available medicine, but more fighting, starvation, and disease. All of these lead to Hell and Death for the people of the earth. This is directly as the seals prophesy. It has all happened in the past, is happening now, and will happen in the future and may be in different stages in different places at any time. This is why we must keep our heads out of the sand and be looking for more than a rapture to magically save us from any troubles.

The opening of the fifth seal is quiet. There is no announcement by anyone. The earth does not even have a clue that it has happened because it marks events in heaven. We are simply introduced to the souls who are underneath the altar in heaven. We are told that they are there, having been slain for the word of God and their testimony. The word cried here means to scream aloud. This crying brings with it both worship to God and questions of the timing of vengeance. They are covered by what symbolically had the blood of sacrifice upon it, the altar. They are then clothed in white robes, which indicates their purity through this blood. Their definition of being souls in the Greek makes them disembodied, so there has been no resurrection of the body. This brings us to a discussion on the much-argued rapture and resurrection and whether they are spiritual or physical. Once again, this debate is rather pointless. We are taught that we shall be as our risen Lord. We will have the nature of both. Christ walked through walls after His resurrection but also ate fish and wore clothes. The disembodied under the altar wear robes but are still waiting on their brethren to be slain as they were. This event is past, present, and future in that there are those who have been slain, are being slain, and will be slain.

The sixth seal is also unannounced. It just catches the earth unaware. Its calamities begin with a great earthquake. The sun goes dark, the moon turns red, stars fall from the sky, and the skies roll back as a scroll. These events can be viewed as seeming natural. They occur on some scales when volcanoes erupt and when large meteorites hit the earth. This has happened on occasions since the writing of John. My personal feeling is that the future event is one caused by an asteroid strike due to the responses of verses 15–17. The great men of the earth hid themselves in the dens and rocks of the mountains. This indicates that there was enough forewarning for the elite that they could make these preparations. The United States has a facility in the Rockies for these types of events already, as do most major world governments.

In Matthew 24:29–31, Jesus gives us the events of the seven seals in their exact order. I believe this is Christ's description of the seals opening. In chapter 7, the 144,000 Jews are sealed for the tribulation to come. Meantime, the earliest possibility for the rapture occurs as witnessed in 7:9. This belief is as I understand not very popular, but even this is probably a premature estimation. In Matthew 24:30–31, we find the trumpet and the cloud sign of His coming, and the book of 1 Thessalonians 4:15–18 also bears this order out. In verse 15, there are some dead already. In 16–17, there is the sign of His coming in the clouds, the archangel, the trumpet, and the dead are already there, and then we are caught up to meet them in the air. Then we are forever with Christ. Revelation 7:9-17 gives us the view of these events from heaven and is the promise given to them under the altar being fulfilled, but realistically we are dying as a people on a regular basis. This makes the way for the wrath of God. To my recollection, these events have not occurred in the past, and we could now assume that the prophetic key for the church is fully inserted into the lock for this series of seven and leave us with the future events for this earth in the soon coming wrath of God.

The seventh seal is found in chapter 8 with a very interesting view of heaven. The place that before was filled with worship, praise, prayers, trumpets, and inquiry is now totally silent for the space of a half an hour. That which has been sealed from the foundations is now open; the lock is turned. Mourning in advance ensues for the inhabitants of the earth as the escalation to the end has been released. The prayers of those upon the earth suffering from the previous seals are not heard. It is but for a heavenly moment and the scroll is opened. Many of the following events have been mirrored in our past. As we have stated throughout this study, it is all in threefold perspective. I will focus primarily on the future wrath. I do realize that Nero fits descriptions given after this point, even down to the numeric value of his name. Some events mirror Antiochus Epiphany. We are taught by Christ that there shall be many antichrists along the way. I believe that there is a big one yet to come upon the earth, one who is the great liar. He may even be preparing today for his time. We cannot be sure of when or who, but we should be sober minded and prepared.

The seventh seal brings with it a view of seven angels with seven trumpets. If it is true that seven is symbolic if completion, it would feel in good company here as three sevens are revealed. Another angel takes a burning censer full of incense, which is the prayers of the saints upon the golden altar that comes up before God. We saw this clearly in the fifth seal, and the time of the answered prayer is now at hand. This means that their brethren have also departed the earth, but we must remember that they are to be slain. If this is a marker of a previous rapture, then we must assume that the rapture is actually the death of all the saints on the earth. We all have a personal rapture date appointed unto us. In Hebrews 9:27, we are told that it is "appointed" for men to once die and then to be judged. This censer is cast into the earth after being loaded with holy fire from the altar. The righteous answer of God for the prayers of the saints has begun with a strike from the heavens which opens up sounds and events not previously heard or seen. Voices, thundering, lightning, and an earthquake come to life before the trumpets even sound. We see that the nature of God is to answer our prayers in the time that it will be answered appropriately. His answer then will be perfect even if we think it may be late. The wait is worth it.

The scroll of the prewritten wrath of God is now completely unhindered, and we patiently wait for the declaration of His wrath. This is not a reactive measure of God, but rather it is prescribed. Our God of all knows all and accurately warns us by prophecy. Christ is proved worthy through His perfect testimony, and God is proved righteous through the sending of the sacrifice in the way of His only begotten Son. Jesus shows us in John 3 that He came not to condemn the world but that it was already condemned, as this is the nature of this scroll. The earths suffering at the beginning of the end is marked by seven trumpets, and the first four are as follows: (1) one-third of plant life is burned up, (2) one-third of the sea becomes as blood, killing one-third of all life, including sailors in the sea, (3) one-third of fresh water is made bitter, and (4) one-third of all natural light is darkened, including the sun, moon, and stars.

The fifth trumpet marks the beginning of the three woes that were announced in chapter 8:13. Up to this point, all thee occurrences of the seals and trumpets could be perceived as natural events. We see horrific things at the hand of nature regularly. I believe that the world as a whole is probably still trying to make sense of these occurrences. These woes, however, bring with them an unmistakable air of the supernatural. The world is about to meet the one they have served in ignorance. With this first woe there falls from heaven a star that opens the bottomless pit, releasing, amongst other things, additional darkness as the sun and moon are covered by a cloud of smoke. Only the 144,000 sealed Jews are not tormented by some previously unknown pest that brings five months of illness but not death. Verse six says that the torture is so bad that man will seek death and not find it. The description of these creatures of torment makes one think of the unnatural origin of such a creature. Despite all the conjecture over what John saw, all of this reeks of supernatural problems. Finally, as a part of this woe, we are introduced to the earth's new problem, Satan in the flesh, answering to Apollyon or Abaddon. He is the king of the creatures of this woe, which inclines me to believe that his demons are released in physical form. Their ultimate goal is the driving of humanity to the worship of Satan.

The sixth trumpet has the second woe attached. Four angels are released from confinement in the Euphrates River and will slay one-third of the remaining population. This is drastically affecting the infrastructure of the earth. Death is hard to deal with when one knows one's fate, but in this case of horror that the earth is suffering in the loss of the bands of family and friend will become devastating to the morale of man. There is suffering with no death, followed by sudden death by slaying. Some ask why God is training angels to do such harm, but prepare means that these angels were already set for this course. God's mercy has held them back for the duration from the time of the expelling from the Garden of Eden. God is giving man what he has always wanted— independence. Another third are slain at the hands of some two hundred million horsemen of some other supernatural description that carries with it much speculation and pointless argument. What is important is that the remaining independent strong humanists of the world are worshipping devils and idols of many descriptions and continue in gross sin against God and self.

Another angel is brought into view as John stands in awe. This angel is described as a mighty being that carries a little book. There are many explanations for the appearance of this angel, varying by what meanings there are for the symbolic nature of him. Just striking is sufficient for me. Standing on water and earth can indicate anything from the fact that he is not subject to the rules of our nature to simply being representative of the universality of his message. He roars as he speaks and when seven thunders speak a reply, John being a good steward of his duty begins to write but is instructed to stop. Remember that in chapter 1 John was instructed to write what he sees and not all that he hears. This one little thing makes it impossible for us to fully understand the entirety of this prophecy of the wrath of God. After this, however, the angel swears that there will be no further delay in the completion of the mystery of God. This being a mystery could not be written by John. It is declared to his prophets, but not to mankind. John is not the only one being quiet, as all prophecy apparently falls under this precept. Jesus tells us in Matthew 7:6 not to cast our pearls before swine, lest they trample them underfoot and turn and rend you. There are some things that cannot be received by mankind. Upon John's eating of the little book, we find it sweet to the mouth but bitter to the belly, and John is then required to continue to prophesy. It is sweet to taste God's righteousness in His judgment but bitter to see the suffering of these "peoples, and nations, and tongues, and kings."

The city of Jerusalem is the venue of the continuation of woe. The temple is measured as to the inner court. It is really hard to measure what does not exist. We assume that by the time of the second woe the temple is reconstructed. I would assume that the mosque that currently occupies this spot is destroyed during the previous earthquakes. The outer court is given to the Gentiles for a time frame of three and one half years. It is this timeframe that ties Daniel to Revelation. Most students of the tribulation use this to make an even break of seven years. The two prophets are given 1,260 days to prophecy, which is also three and one half years. They are protected by supernatural power. Most postulate that these two are Moses and Elijah. If this is a literal happening, I would probably pick Enoch and Elijah, as neither has yet tasted death and speak from both sides of Noah's flood. Revelation does teach us that they can perform plague and drought as often as they desire. This power, as well as the message that they bring, causes the world to cheer as these two are finally slain at the hands of the beast of the pit. This wins the hearts of the people to this beast. These two prophets are reanimated, and at such time the second woe ends.

The beginning of the third woe is trumpeted in with the seventh and final trumpet. In 1 Corinthians 15:51–58 we see a declaration of the last trumpet as the call of the saints to heaven. Interestingly, this verse is one of the benchmarks of the pretribulational teachers, but the "trumpet" of Revelation 4:1 is the first "trumpet," not the last as indicated by 1 Corinthians 15. If we insist on Revelation being literal, then we need to be open to the fact that this is the last trumpet, and although we hope differently, this could very well be the rapture of the church. In fact, there is more evidence to this end as to either of the two previous assertions of a rapture of the church. In further support of this, in verse 18 we see the heavenly declaration of the wrath to come. We are redirected to heaven to find the elders worshipping in a declaration of expression of the actions of God as He is taking up His power to reign. The nature of these elders is always in harmony to the events of heaven. The servants in white are not attached to this. I would surmise that these elders predate the earth as we know it. We should not think too highly of ourselves, as our physical form is of dust and returns to it. We know by the worship of the elders that all creation is about God, not man. It also has taken no archeological journey to find the Ark of the Covenant. It is in the heavenly temple where it has always been. What was upon this earth was but a replica. We should not allow any find of the earthly one to awe us, as the power was of God, not of the ark. There is much activity around the ark, which is very mystical to us. God's current representation of the Ark of the Covenant lies within us. He chooses to empower us to represent Him. The prophets' and apostles' powers reflect God's control of them. We also need to be where we are supposed to be at the time He wants us there if we are to see the working of His power in us. Simply, seek God's will for your life and you will experience the move of His spirit upon you.

Chapter 12 is an exquisite view of a summary of the war in heaven done in symbolic detail and can represent a change in the course of this book. The book of Job is a work of dramatic poetry that teaches us of the plight of man, the righteousness of God, the suffering of the righteous, the overcoming of the faithful, and the reward of God. Verse 18 of chapter 11 shows us the mind-set of heaven. Chapter 12 is a dramatic and informative story that shows us the character of Satan and the plight of the earth. There are again many different takes upon this story, ranging from it being just a nice story all the way to a very literal belief that this happens in the last days with a real dragon. I view it as the big picture set in drama. God is good and wants to bring forth good. Satan is evil and does not care who gets destroyed, including all of creation. Briefly, 1–2 introduce us to the heritage of the promise to Abraham from Genesis 22:17–18. Israel is the lineage from which the Son of man must come to bless the entire world. Satan, who is already at war with God, does all that he can to stop the redemption of man in

3–4. In 5, we find that the man child Christ is successful in birth, death, and resurrection. Verse six shows us the 144,000 sealed Jews being protected for 1,260 days or three and one half years. In 7–9, we see the continuing uprising of Satan and his ultimate failure. Verses 10–11 indicate the loss of Satan's ability to accuse the saved of Christ. Verse 12 is the third woe of Satan being in the earth with but a short time. In 13–17, Satan is persecuting the remnant of the seed of Abraham who is protected for three and one half years.

A confederacy of nations is found in the beginning of chapter 13 that is represented by the unity of the different beasts. By verse 11, this political union is married with religion to make a one-world government. Think back to Laodicea with their wealth and medicine. They were the crossroads of the world. They are lukewarm and can cause no discomfort to evil. This coupled with the thought of economic equality (vs. 17) among the much-diminished population of the world is enough to lure in most people. Once again, we come to a much-debated and popular part of this book. The number of the beast (666) is the mathematical language equivalent for Nero Caesar. In Daniel 3 there is an idol that was 60 cubits high by 6 in breadth. If breadth is considered square to depth, then it is 6x6x60 in the measure of a man. Some say that symbolically six is the number of Satan. The really important part is that we understand that this is the number of a man. It also is important to understand that if the pretibulationalist and midtribulationalist are wrong about the rapture and the amillenialist are wrong about the symbolism of this book, that we all may have this option of a mark given to us. That sounds scary, but the fact is that if we steadfastly follow God and take no marks upon our souls, then we should not take the one that is upon the flesh. Regardless of our belief system, it all boils down to trusting our Lord and Savior. In light of this option, we should remember not to place our trust in the government of man, whether in church or state, because this beast will be a chief, president, or prime minister in the public eye that will court religion if not thrive in it.

    Chapter 14 brings us to light on the happenings of chapter 12. The 144,000 are redeemed from the earth, having finally been slain by the dragon. This means that the three and one half years has expired. They are the first fruits of this order of time. In verse 6, an angel flies through the heavens preaching the gospel to all mankind. It is a gospel of resistance to the beast and his number that includes a blessing within death for those that refuse it. The awaited time is now at hand. Chapter 15 is the opening of the seven vials of the last plagues of the wrath of God. Verses 2–4 show us the saved in death worshipping before God. Praise God that we have the salvation of life. Not everyone has it as easy as we have it. Vials 1–6 are as follows: (1) bad sores, (2) the seas turned completely to blood, with the death of all therein, (3) all fresh water is made blood, (4) increased solar heat to the point of scorching, (5) blinding pain, and (6) the complete drying of the Euphrates River. Satan utilizes three unclean spirits to perform miracles before the rulers of the world in order to rally the troops unto Armageddon. These miracles are probably some form of relief to those who are afflicted. The seventh vial that has been reserved is now emptied, and a voice declares the end of the time of the Gentiles. There is also a similar occurrence as with the Ark of the Covenant in many voices being heard, but we have prayed as Christ instructed, "Thy will be done, in earth as it is in heaven." This is followed by the biggest earthquake that ever occurs. The islands of the sea are sunk, the mountains are flattened, and hail of enormous size afflicts mankind.

In 16:19, we see that Babylon is brought into remembrance before God. In chapter 17, it is portrayed as a harlot with the name "Mystery, Babylon the Great, the mother of harlots and abominations of the earth." This Babylon is not a simple thing. It is a mystery and not completely understandable. It is an occurrence, an idea, a theology, a mind-set, and theme as much as it is a country or city. This began at the tower of Babel. This is where the name is derived. This is the unification of man, government, and religion against the one true God. This is the mother of open wickedness of the post-flood era of the earth. The results of this lifestyle are always the same. She is riding the beast in the last days. This shows us the nature of the beast as well. They together are the combined spirit of antichrist in worship and rule. The beast, having the symbolism of the heads and horns, shows the mixing of heritage and governments. There are problems in this one- world system of government that are done away with by the destruction of this harlot by the beast. Secular humanism is not even tolerated by Satan. Man is made a little lower than the angels, and Satan is an angel cast down. He will not share his throne. It is truly the worship of self that has fueled the riches of the kingdoms of earth. The Laodicean trust in riches and self is rewarded as God said in Revelation 3:16 by being spewed out of the mouth of God. The people traded their souls for the illusion.

We find the marriage supper announced in chapter 19. Christ comes back to earth upon His horse and dispatches the beast and the false prophet to the lake of fire. He kills the remnant of the people that stood against Him with the word of His mouth. This is followed by the binding of Satan in the pit for another thousand years. This marks the beginning of the millennial reign of Christ. There is much debate on whether this is symbolic, the present, or a future event. As this study goes, it is a time in the future that we have not yet seen. I believe that Christ will rule a new earth age over the remnant repopulated onto the earth and the children left from the time of wrath. The antediluvian world was saved in a remnant of Noah and family. Remember that we are told that Christ will rule with a rod of iron. The destructions of the wrath of God are forgotten and there is an uprising against the capital of Jerusalem by nations of the earth with the release of Satan from his pit and his continuing deception. The uprising is consumed in fire, and the devil is cast into the lake of fire for eternal torment. The Great White Throne is revealed, as are the books of the deeds of man and the Book of Life. All the dead that have ever been stand before God to answer for their deeds. Only the ones in the Lamb's Book of Life are spared from the lake of fire.

Finally

In chapter 20, we saw the ultimate end. Finally now in chapter 21, we see the ultimate beginning. There is a new heaven and a new earth. There will be a New Jerusalem. There will be new bodies and new innocence. There will be no temple, sun, or moon. Thirst, hunger, heat, cold, and dark will be no more. All these are wonderful, tangible reasons to want to be with Jesus Christ. Verse 11 gives us the greatest reason to follow Him. It is a permanent abode. We are warned in 18–19 not to add to or take away from this book. I have friends and fellows who all take this book differently, as I have previously stated. I would love to think that Jesus is going to rapture us before the tribulation, but this may not be the case. I would love to think that this book is strictly historic to us, and that we are just biding our time till His kingdom is revealed. This may not be either. I can, however, after studying this book, as well as the whole Bible, guarantee you a few things. God is righteous, as well as right. He will win and has won. God is merciful, His grace is sufficient, and following Christ is worth it all. Eternity is a really long time, and I want to spend it with Him! Don't you?

Appendix I

A Premillenial Timeline

1. Revelation 1:1—3:13
(The past ages of the church)

2. Revelation 3:14–22
(Laodicea or the current church age)

3. Revelation 4:1–2
(The rapture of the church and first resurrection of the saints)

4. Revelation 5:1–14
(The future presentation of the scroll to Christ)

5. Revelation 6:1
(The start of the seven-year great tribulation
by the opening of the first seal)

6. Revelation 6:2—9:21
(The first three and a half years marked with the wrath of God)

7. Revelation 10
(The symbolic start of the last three and a half years)

8. Revelation 11
(The institution of a new temple in Jerusalem
and the prophets Moses and Elijah)

9. Revelation 12
(A war in heaven brought to earth)

10. Revelation 13; Revelation 14:9–11
(The revelation of the antichrist and the mark of the beast)

11. Revelation 14:1–7
(The sealing of 144,000 Jews to preach the gospel)

12. Revelation 14:8; Revelation 17:1—18:24
(The fall of a Babylon of disputed identity)

13. Revelation 14:12—16:15
(The second wrath and the first battle of man against God)

14. Revelation 16:16–21
(The battle of Armageddon)

15. Revelation 19:1–16
(The coming of the saints with Christ
And the second resurrection of the tribulational saints)

16. Revelation 19:17—20:2
(The battle of the saints and Christ against the earth)

17. Revelation 20:3–6
(The millennial reign of Christ and His saints)

18. Revelation 20:7–9
(The battle against Gog and Magog against God)

19. Revelation 20:10–15
(The final resurrection and Great White Throne Judgment)

20. Revelation 21:1—eternity
(The new eternal glory and condition of the saints)

Appendix II

A Mid-tribulational Timeline

1. Revelation 1:1—3:7
(The past church ages)

2. Revelation 3:8–22
(The current church age
and the beginning of the tribulation)

3. Revelation 4:1—14:20
(The various, escalating events of the beginning
of the tribulation, both literal and symbolic,
including historical symbolisms)

4. Revelation 15:1—16:15
(The entrance of the saints of the rapture
and the first resurrection of the saints
along with the marked beginning
of the great wrath of God and the
beginning of the three-and-a-half-year great tribulation)

5. Revelation 16:16–21
(The battle of Armageddon)

6. Revelation 19:1–16
(The coming of the saints with Christ)

7. Revelation 19:17—20:2
(The battle of the saints and Christ against the earth)

8. Revelation 20:3–6
(The millennial reign of Christ and His saints)

9: Revelation 20:7–9
(The battle against Gog and Magog against God)

10: Revelation 20:10–15
(The great resurrection and Great White Throne Judgment)

11: Revelation 21:1—eternity
(The new eternal glory and condition of the saints)

Appendix III

An Amillenial Timeline

1. Revelation 1
(The establishment of a historic and symbolic account)

2. Revelation 2:1—3:22
(A group of seven historic but applicable epistles)

3. Revelation 4:1—20:10
(A symbolic account of historic and prophetical occurrences both from the fulfilling of Daniel and the end)

4. Revelation 20:11–15
(The first and only resurrection, also known as the General Resurrection)

5. Revelation 21 & 22
(The symbolic representation of the eternity of the saints)

✥

Appendix IV

The Author's Timeline

1. Revelation 2:1–29
(The previous church ages)

2. Revelation 3:1–22
(The current three church ages)

3. Revelation 4:1–11
(The currently opened seals of the symbolic scroll
and the continual cycle presented in these seals
always starting with war and ending
in the oppression of the saints)

4. Revelation 4:12–17
(The currently unopened seal)

5. Revelation 5:1—11:14
(The quickly cascading events of the symbolic seven trumpets
that shall happen as the culmination of the seventh seal,
along with the seven hidden symbolic thunders
and the two prophets representing Enoch,
who was translated before the Great Flood,
and Elijah, who was translated after)

6. Revelation 11:15–19
(The "rapture" of the church)

7. Revelation 12–18
(The time of the symbolic beast, the blinded Laodicean church, and the beginning of the wrath of God)

8. Revelation 19:1—20:2
(The symbolic return of the 144,000 to rule with Christ)

9. Revelation 20:3–4
(The inhabitants of the earth during the millennial reign of Christ and the 144,000 Jews)

10. Revelation 20:7–10
(The last stand against God and rejection of His grace)

11. Revelation 20:11–15
(The Great White Throne Judgment and the resurrection mentioned in 20:5–6, before which all shall stand and be separated to their eternal abode)

12. Revelation 21:1—eternity
(The picture of the resurrected earth, heaven, and body. All are new and unblemished from our current condition, and are eternal, sufficient, glorious, and worth the price)

Printed in the USA
CPSIA information can be obtained
at www.ICGtesting.com
LVHW040238040324
773467LV00008B/226